WHAT IS YOUR GOD LIKE?

Gerard W. Hughes

Series editor Jeanne Hinton

To Ursula, whose God brings light from darkness,
laughter from tears, and joy from sorrow.

Copyright © 1994 Hunt & Thorpe
Text © Gerard Hughes
Cover Illustration © Len Munnik

ISBN 1 85608 108 7

Scripture quotations from the Jerusalem Bible – Readers Edition, 1968

In Australia this book is published by:
Hunt & Thorpe Australia Pty Ltd.
9 Euston Street, Rydalmere NSW 2116

A CIP catalogue record for this book is available from the British Library.

Manufactured in the United Kingdom

CONTENTS

■ INTRODUCTION

The 1960s were years of the counter-culture, of
The Beatles, hippies and student unrest, when
everything was being questioned, including God.
I was then teaching at Stonyhurst, a Jesuit public
school. It was a bastion of Catholic orthodoxy,
yet in the classrooms an increasing number of the
pupils were professing atheism. When I was
discussing this problem one day with the
headmaster, he sighed and said, 'I think we
should abolish the name of God'. As I returned
to my room to prepare yet another religion class,
I did not find his comment helpful.

Twenty-five years later, I was staying in
Northern Ireland, discussing the troubles with a
Roman Catholic priest. He, too, sighed and said,
'The only solution is to close down all churches
for 30 years!'

Why abolish the name of God and close down
all the churches for 30 years? Atheists would
answer, 'Because religion causes murderous
divisions between peoples and within individuals.'

Some believers would answer, 'Because our images of God are so deformed that we need to find a new language for religion and a new word for God. Most churches confirm us in our distorted notions of God, and these distorted images deform us, alienating us from ourselves and from one another.'

'What is your God like?' Our answer to this question affects every aspect of our lives. The answer can blight or enrich, deaden or enliven. The purpose of this book is to encourage you to ask this question for yourself. Exercises are offered at the end of each chapter. Your responses may well be the most valuable part of the book for you.

I hope and pray that your search for an answer will bring you to a knowledge of God like that described in section four.

■ 1

DOES IT MATTER?

> O religion, what evils are committed in your name
> Lucretius (1st century BC)

A CONSTANT temptation in every religion, including Christianity, is to usurp God in the name of God and commit crimes in God's name. Every Christian country honours the millions who were killed in its wars, declaring that they died for God and country, as though God were the preserve of a particular nation.

The Christian crusaders believed that by killing Muslims, whom they called 'the Infidel', they were promoting the kingdom of Christ.

The Inquisitors thought they were serving God by burning heretics at the stake.

The Protestant reformers believed they were advancing the cause of religion by hanging, drawing and quartering Catholics, and when the Catholics came to power they did the same to Protestants.

Apartheid lasted for so long in South Africa because the white Dutch Reformed Church believed that Apartheid was a divine command. Members of the Church who questioned the doctrine were excommunicated.

Today, although religion is not the whole cause, it played a very significant part in the terror that reigned in the Lebanon, has been raging in Bosnia and, to a lesser extent, in Northern Ireland.

Why drag up all these objections to God and to religion? Because the evils done in God's name by others, in the past and at present, can also be done by us. It is easy to look with horror at all that Christians have done in God's name in the past: it is more difficult to recognise these same tendencies in ourselves today.

Today, in Britain, all politicians who hope to win an election, and the majority of Christians and of Christian leaders, advocate nuclear deterrence as part of our national defence policy. Initially, nuclear deterrence was considered a necessary defence against the Communist threat. The threat no longer exists, but we still maintain the nuclear deterrent and we have four Trident submarines on order as part of our defence policy. One Trident submarine contains many times more firepower than the total firepower used in the Second World War. The weapons are designed to be first strike weapons, and they could devastate every major city in Europe, killing millions, maiming millions, deforming future generations, besides doing incalculable damage to our planet. Future generations of Christians may well look back on the second half of the 20th century with shame and horror, amazed that Christians and Christian leaders could ever have tolerated such a life-destroying policy.

So far we have looked at the divisions religion can cause between nations, but the division is not only between nations, but between and within churches and families; it can enter into the very soul of individuals. In fact, it is division within the individual that leads to the divisions between groups and nations.

■ OLD UNCLE GEORGE

We are not born with a ready-made notion of
God. We can only come to know God, as we
come to know anything else, through others: our
parents, teachers, preachers, books and religious
services. In the late 1960s, when I was a chaplain
at Glasgow University, I spent many hours with
people who had either rejected God or were
seriously considering doing so.

After many conversations, an identikit picture
of God came to me. It is as though as little
children our loving parents take us to visit 'Good
Old Uncle George', the family's favourite
relative, a man of great wealth and influence. Our
parents tell us that he lives to help us all. Uncle
George, an elderly, bearded and forbidding man,
lives in a large and gloomy mansion.

One day, at the end of your visit, Uncle
George turns to you and declares, 'I want you to
visit me here regularly, and if you fail to come,
let me show you what will happen.' He leads
you down to the mansion's basement, which is
overheated. He opens a steel door and there you
see row upon row of blazing furnaces where

innumerable men, women and children are being hurled into the ovens by little demons. 'And that,' says Uncle George, 'is what will happen to you if you do not visit me regularly.'

You go upstairs to your parents and clutch at them in terror. On the way home, Mummy leans over and says, 'And don't you love Uncle George with all your heart and soul and mind and strength?'

Remembering the furnaces, you lie and say, 'Yes, I do', but you loathe Uncle George and consider him a monster. The lie becomes part of your life, so that you continue to profess love of Uncle George, visit him dutifully, say all the right things to him about how wonderful he is and how grateful you are for his kindness, but deep in your soul you detest him and want nothing to do with him.

■ GOD UNDER MY THUMB

'Uncle George' is one caricature of a deformed image of God, which can blight our lives, but there are many variations. Our notion of God may be that of a genuinely loving father, or mother, or uncle figure, who is always nice to us, always on our side, but seems to have very little interest in anyone or anything else. Such an image of God can confirm us in our deep rooted selfishness and self-righteousness. This is the god of many enthusiastic sects and church groups, who are only interested in their own salvation and comfort. They feel it is their God-given task to keep themselves apart from the contaminating influences of other people who do not belong to their church, sect, or group.

■ GOD LOVES ME IF...

Another image is of a God who approves of us only in so far as we renounce all self-interest and devote ourselves entirely to the service of others. Who sees every trace of weariness as a sign of self-preoccupation, and any delight a self-indulgence which must be overcome.

■ GOD IN A BOX

All these distorted images are of a God who is an 'out-there' God. Whether we think of him as a punishing God, or as a God who only gives gifts to us and the likes of us, or as a God who demands total selflessness, he is a God who is remote from our everyday lives.

What have we done with God? We have compartmentalised him, confining him to the sacred, so leaving us free to get on with the secular, which occupies most of our time, energy and interest. Our language itself expresses this split. We distinguish between supernatural and natural, grace and nature, heavenly and earthly, sacred and profane, in such a way that we come to think of God as outside of our world and its activities. As Christians we believe that God has come to us in Jesus, but we even manage so to present Jesus that his humanity is of very minor importance in comparison with his divinity!

Here is an exercise you can practise on your own. Imagine there is a ring at your front door one evening. When you answer, on the doorstep is the Risen Lord himself. You know without any shadow of doubt that it is the Risen Lord. How do you receive him? Do you tell him to come back on Sunday, or give him directions to the nearest church? Presumably you welcome him in and invite everyone within reach to come and meet him – and find yourself saying ridiculous things like 'do make yourself at home' to the Lord of all Creation – and he gratefully accepts your invitation.

Now imagine your home two weeks later. How is it? To help your imagination you may recall the Gospel passage when Jesus said, 'It is not peace I have come to bring, but a sword... to set son against father, daughter against mother, daughter-in-law against mother-in-law...' (Matthew 10:34-36) What has been happening over the last fortnight at family meals? Who has been leaving the table suddenly and slamming doors, and why?

As you have invited Jesus to make himself at home, he has been inviting his friends. Who were Jesus' friends in the Gospels, and what kind of people are arriving at your home? What are the neighbours saying, and what is happening to local property values?

You take Jesus to the local church to give a talk to a gathering of parishioners. You remember the little talk he gave to the chief priests, scribes and Pharisees, in which he assured them that the tax collectors and prostitutes would get into the kingdom of God before they did? He gives substantially the same talk in the parish church and there is uproar, the parish losing its principal benefactors.

You return home with Jesus and ponder your problem. You cannot get rid of him, for he is Lord of all Creation. So you look around the house, find a suitable cupboard, clear, clean and decorate it, and have a good strong lock put on it. You can then put Jesus inside, lock the door and place a lamp and flowers in front of it. Each time you pass, you make a deep reverential bow. You now have Jesus where you want him and he does not interfere any more!

Is this what we have done with Jesus and with God, locked them away safely so that they do not interfere with our everyday lives, while paying them outward forms of reverence, believing that if we do this, all will be well?

■ EXERCISES FOR SECTION I

1. Try for yourself the imaginative exercise described above.

2. A useful way of discovering your own image of God is to try the following exercise, writing out the answers:

a. What image of God was presented to you in the past?

b. What is your present image of God?

c. How would you like God to be?

2

GLIMPSING GOD IN HIS CREATION

BEFORE ASKING 'what is God like?', we need first to ask 'is there a God?' A starting point is to change the question to 'is there a power greater than myself?', because many people who profess not to believe in God are merely rejecting the image of God they were presented with in childhood. I have had many conversations with people who professed to be atheist. What they were rejecting was their perceived image of God. Real atheists are rare.

It is natural and healthy that we should question the notion of God as it has been presented to us. We may find that this is an invitation from God to discover him for ourselves. God is truth. Those who reject childish notions of God are moving nearer to him, not rejecting him.

We can only come to a knowledge of God

through our own experience: we have no other option. Does our experience lead us to acknowledge 'a power greater than myself', or to deny such a possibility? The answer depends on our definition of experience. If we decide that nothing can exist that cannot be objectively proved, then God cannot exist, because God is not an object that can be verified. The criterion we have set rules out God.

That is why the atheist is as dogmatic as any fundamentalist believer. Agnostics are more modest: having surveyed reality, they conclude that there is no way of knowing whether God exists, or not. As we shall see, there must always be a large element of agnosticism in any true believer. The believer knows there is 'a power greater than myself', but acknowledges his or her great ignorance of the nature of God.

■ VAST BEYOND IMAGINING

Is there a power greater than myself? The psalmist says, 'I look up at your heavens, shaped by your fingers, at the moon and the stars you set firm.' (Psalm 8:3) A good starting point is to look at the heavens. Our planet earth is a tiny dot in our galaxy and our galaxy a very tiny dot in the universe. So far, astronomers have been able to make out objects up to ten billion light years away, which means that if we were to travel at the speed of light, at 186, 282 miles per second, it would take us ten billion years to reach what is at present the furthest visible object.

One astronomer, writing in 1984, has stated,

'Even conservative astronomers are now facing up to the remarkable discovery that even quite nearby regions of space must contain between ten and a hundred times more mass than we can presently account for. Around and between galaxies like our Milky Way, space appears to be dominated by massive invisible agencies which defy our efforts at detection and mock our present theories of the Universe. We now find ourselves in a Universe largely inhabited by invisible agencies whose nature we can only wonder at.'
    The Guardian 18 October 1984

J. B. Haldane said, 'The universe is proving to be not only more mysterious than we imagine but even more mysterious than we ever could imagine.' It does not seem unreasonable to suppose that there is 'a power greater than myself'?

■ COMPLEX BEYOND COMPREHENDING

When we focus our attention not on the heavens, but on our own bodies, the wonder intensifies. Our own bodies consist largely of empty space. If we could see ourselves through a sufficiently powerful microscope we would discover that we consist of billions of cells, each cell as intricate in its formation as a galaxy, each cell containing sufficient information to reconstruct the whole body.

Most of us have no awareness of these cells, a merciful ignorance! We find an ordinary day's work quite stressful enough without having to regulate the six trillion chemical changes per second which, it is reckoned, occur in the human body!

■ A MYSTERIOUS UNITY

The atom is not the ultimate particle of matter, as the ancients believed, but is in itself highly complex. Its components are not elementary particles of matter, things which collectively assemble to form bigger things, but a network of relations, an inseparable web of vibrating energy patterns in which no one component has reality independent of the entirety. One scientist has summarised this conclusion in the phrase,

'Every particle consists of every other particle'

which sounds more like the utterance of a mystic than the conclusion of a nuclear scientist.

If this is the case, then every action of ours has reverberations throughout creation. When a baby throws its rattle out of the cradle the planets rock, or, as the poet Francis Thompson wrote:

All things by immortal power
Near or far
Hiddenly, to each other linked are
That thou canst not stir a flower
Without trembling a star
    (The Mistress of Vision)

It is not only our physical actions that have an effect throughout the universe. The very observation of an electron, for example, can change its direction, and that change will be balanced by a corresponding change, perhaps thousands of miles away. Until recently scientists thought that nothing could travel faster than light, but now they believe there is something much faster. The Buddhists have been teaching this doctrine for centuries, believing that the peaceful and loving aspirations of the heart go out in waves and can affect all creation instantly. Christian tradition has always encouraged us to believe that prayer can be effective throughout the world.

Pondering these truths, it is not unreasonable to assert that there is 'a power greater than myself'; or, to put it another way, that I am part of something much greater than me. It is extraordinarily arrogant and stupid to assert that there can be no such power. But what is the nature of this power? Is it benevolent or malevolent, capricious or caring, blind or provident?

■ GOD BEYOND

Christian tradition states that God is both transcendent and immanent. Transcendent means that God is always greater than anything we can think or imagine.

> 'My thoughts are not your thoughts, and your ways are not my ways,' declares Yahweh.
>   Isaiah 55:8

So the simple answer to our question, 'what is God like?' is 'God knows', or 'like nothing on earth'.

God is a beckoning word, always leading us beyond the present into an unimaginable future. Of his nature, God cannot be tamed, domesticated, defined or adequately described. To us he is always bound to be unpredictable and surprising. We can have few certainties in this life, but you can be certain of this; if anyone claims to know exactly what God is like and what we must do to find him, you may be sure that person is wrong.

This is a profoundly important truth for every religious person, every Christian church, sect or group. Had we respected the transcendence of God and therefore questioned our religious certainties in the past, many lives would have been saved and much misery avoided.

■ GOD WITHIN

But God is also immanent, that is, God is in all things. St Paul, speaking in Athens, quoted a Greek poet and said of God, 'It is in him that we live, and move, and exist.' (Acts 17:28)

Mahomet said that God is nearer to us than our jugular vein, and St. Augustine, 'God is closer to me than I am to myself.'

Annie Besant wrote of the immanence of God:

> O Hidden Life, vibrant in every atom,
> O Hidden Light, shining in every creature,
> O Hidden Love, embracing all in Oneness,
> May each who feels himself as one with Thee
> Know He is therefore one with every other.

There is no place, no circumstance, in which God is not present. He cannot be locked in cupboards or confined to churches, chapels and shrines. As the psalmist said, we cannot escape from his presence:

> Where shall I go to escape your spirit?
> Where shall I flee from your presence?
> If I scale the heavens, you are there,
> If I lie flat in She'ol, there you are.
>
> If I speed away on the wings of the dawn,
> If I dwell beyond the ocean,
> even there your hand will be guiding me,
> your right hand holding me fast.
>   Psalm 139:7–10

We are taught that we find God in prayer, in church, in receiving the sacraments, but we are in God whatever we do and, as far as God is concerned, he is as near to us when we sleep, eat, or go to the loo, as he is when we pray.

■ TWO DANGERS

As Christians our temptation is to emphasise the transcendence of God and forget his immanence, or to emphasise his immanence and forget his transcendence.

The remote God

Those who emphasise God's transcendence will concentrate on specifically religious things. They will have elaborate, well ordered and beautiful liturgies, which emphasise the otherness, and mystery of God, but their services and prayers will tend to have little to do with everyday life.

Politics, social structures, economic and defence policies will not be a matter of religious concern, and the spirituality of any who are interested in these matters will be suspect. This tendency to overemphasise the transcendence of God to the detriment of his immanence is widespread in our country, where the majority of Christians and Christian leaders are supporters of a nuclear deterrence policy. They will pray beautifully for peace, but they will never allow their notion of peace to contaminate their prayer, consequently they can say finely constructed prayers, then behave murderously. Imagine this prayer being uttered in church and the effect it might have on the supporters of nuclear deterrents.

> Dear Lord, inspire our scientists that they may invent yet more lethal weaponry (for the more lethal it is, the more it is likely to deter). Save us from any unfortunate accident in its testing, lest our own land should be devastated. Bless our economy that we may put these weapons into plentiful production. Have a special care of the hungry, homeless and sick of our own and other countries, until such time as our defence commitments allow us to contribute a little more. Strengthen our leaders in a strong defence policy. Drive out from our midst any, who by thought, word or deed, undermine our national security, and protect us with our nuclear arms both now and forever. Amen

The cosy God

Those who emphasise God's immanence will be more casual in their approach to liturgy, ensuring that all prayers have a direct bearing on everyday life and that church music is indistinguishable from secular.

God will be addressed in familiar terms and a substantial amount of time in the Eucharist may be spent in giving one another hugs and kisses. God will be the supporter of whatever preoccupies the congregation, their sense of justice and God's coinciding admirably. The danger is that divine service will lose all sense of mystery and God will be boxed into the mind set of the group or church.

The problem for all of us is to hold God's transcendence and God's immanence in tension. Both are true, but as human beings we can only find God in and through our experience, in and through his immanence, and it is only in his immanence that we can catch a glimpse of his transcendence. Those who try to bypass the immanence and make directly for the transcendence of God will arrive at an abstraction, not the God of Abraham, Isaac and Jacob, and Father of Our Lord Jesus Christ.

But we still do not know what this transcendent and immanent God is like, so now we shall look briefly at the Bible to see how God is described, and what this means for us.

■ EXERCISES FOR SECTION 2

1. We can only come to God through our own experience. In your experience of religion, has God been for you mostly transcendent, mostly immanent, or equally both?

2. How is God for you now?

■ 3

HOW THE BIBLE DESCRIBES GOD

'The whole world, for you, can no more than tip a
balance,
like a drop of morning dew falling on the ground.
Yet you are merciful to all, because you are
almighty.
you overlook people's sins, so that they can repent.
Yes, you love everything that exists,
and nothing that you have made disgusts you,
since, if you had hated anything, you would not
have made it.
And how could a thing subsist, had you not willed
it?
Or how be preserved, if not called forth by you?
No, you spare all, since all is yours, Lord, lover of
life!
For your imperishable spirit is in everything!'
    Wisdom II:22-12:1

This passage shows God's transcendence:

'The whole world, for you, can no more than tip a
balance.'

and God's immanence:

'For your imperishable spirit is in everything.'

When Scripture describes God as holy, the word includes both his transcendence – his otherness – and his immanence, which is characterised by compassion:

> 'You spare all, since all is yours, Lord,
> lover of life!'

■ THE HEBREW PROPHETS

The old Testament teachers, God's spokesmen, describe a transcendent God of awesome power who says,

> 'My ways are above your ways, my thoughts above your thoughts.'

Yet his tender compassion for his people is so great that he enters into a covenant of love with them, sometimes described as a marriage, between God and his people:

> 'I shall betroth you to myself for ever, I shall betroth you in uprightness and justice, and faithful love and tenderness. Yes I shall betroth you to myself in loyalty and in the knowledge of Yahweh.'
> Hosea 2:20-22

God expects his people to be loyal to him, as he is to them. This means that in their lives, in their behaviour to one another and to the stranger, they must reflect his compassion, tenderness and mercy.

When they betray God's love by oppressing, exploiting and destroying his creation, he is furious. The wrath and harshness of God in the Hebrew Scriptures is the obverse of his love. Again and again the Hebrew prophets declare God's compassion for his creation, and his anger against those who profess to worship him but do not mirror his compassion. Here are some examples from Amos, the earliest of the recorded prophets.

Amos was a poor shepherd living in the south at a time when the country was divided. The northern kingdom being affluent and sophisticated, the southern kingdom poor and uncultured. God called Amos to preach in the north. Here he addresses the cultured ladies of Samaria, the northern capital:

'Listen to this saying, you cows of Bashan
living on the hill of Samaria,
exploiting the weak and ill-treating the poor,
saying to your husbands, 'Bring us something to
drink!'
    Amos 4:1

'Because they have sold the upright for silver
and the poor for a pair of sandals,
because they have crushed the heads of the weak
into the dust
and thrust the rights of the oppressed to one side...
I shall crush you where you stand.'
    Amos 2:6-7,13

The people to whom these words are addressed
are a religious people, who worship regularly.
Amos comments on their religious services:

I hate, I scorn your festivals,
I take no pleasure in your solemn assemblies...
Spare me the din of your chanting,
Let me hear none of your strumming on lyres,
But let justice flow like water,
And uprightness like a never-failing stream!
    Amos 5:21-24

So what is God like according to the Old
Testament? He is a God who has entered into a
covenant, a marriage with Israel. This covenant is
not with Israel only: it is a covenant with all
creation, but Israel is to be 'the light of the
nations'. Faithfulness to the covenant demands
that Israel should reflect in her behaviour the
justice and compassion of God, not only within
Israel, but also to the stranger. Failure to do this

is infidelity. There can be no peace for the nation unless it is mirroring the justice, compassion and integrity of Yahweh.

We read the Scriptures to help us to recognise God now, in our century, in our circumstances. We read the Hebrew prophets because their message is an eternal one, that is, it is always applicable to the present. The prophets always addressed their message to the nation, not to individuals, except as representatives of the nation, so we have to hear these words addressed to us today as a nation.

■ JESUS

The characteristic of Jesus' life that distinguishes him from every other great religious leader is his relationship to God, whom he calls 'Abba', a child's name for father.

Whatever he sees, whether sparrows, lilies, crops being sown, sheep, fruit on trees, withered branches, landscape, the colour and shape of clouds, human faces, dress or human conventions, he sees in relation to his Father,

who pervades his being as yeast pervades dough,
salt permeates meat, light penetrates darkness.

Jesus' stories

What is the Father like for Jesus? The parables
give us a clue: it is the stories people tell that
reveal their inner minds and hearts. One of Jesus'
favourite images of God's kingdom is the image
of the wedding feast. In one parable God is
represented as a king who gives a feast for his
son's wedding. The father's one anxiety is that as
many people as possible should come. When
some refuse the invitation, he tells his servants to
go out into the highways and byways and bring
them all in – the poor, the crippled, the lame and
the blind. In Matthew's Gospel the servants are
told to bring in everyone 'bad and good alike',
which is very comforting! So God is represented
as a God of overflowing goodness.

According to St Thomas Aquinas, the great
medieval theologian, creation happened because
it is in the nature of goodness to overflow. The
only people who incur God's anger are those
who refuse his generosity, or prevent others from
enjoying it.

When the Pharisees objected to Jesus' behaviour, complaining that he kept bad company, Jesus told them three parables which describe what God is like (Luke 15). The first is the parable of the lost coin, the second the parable of the lost sheep, and the third is the parable called the prodigal son, though it is a parable of two sons, both lost but in different ways. The father of the prodigal son freely allows his son to go off and enjoy himself, then waits longingly for his boy to return. When eventually 'he sees him from afar', he rushes out to greet him. The boy tries to explain that he has sinned against God and his father, but the father seems to ignore the confession, embraces his son, kisses him, gives him a ring, a robe and sandals for his feet and orders the fattened calf to be killed. It is an extraordinary picture of God, a God who is foolish by our standards, permissive and, like his son, prodigal.

He is foolish, too, in leaving the ninety-nine sheep to go after the one that is lost. How much more prudent the Church has been in her history!

In the parables, God is presented as financially imprudent, a God who would not fare well in a world of market forces! He forgives one debtor ten thousand talents, equivalent to a few million pounds, but then gets into a rage when that same debtor tries to extort a few pence from a debtor of his (Matthew 18:23-35). God cannot stand stinginess.

One of the most disturbing parables is the parable of the rich man and a beggar called Lazarus (Luke 16:19-31). There is no evidence that the wealthy Dives oppresses Lazarus or maltreats him. It is Dives' failure to notice that incurs God's wrath. It is a sobering parable when we look, or fail to look, at the homelessness and poverty today in our own country and at the destitution that millions suffer because of our nation's lifestyle.

Jesus' lifestyle

So the God of Jesus is a God who, by our standards, is lavish, prodigal and foolish in his generosity. Jesus revealed this God not only in every word he spoke but in his actions. He said,

'Anyone who has seen me has seen the Father.' (John 14:9) It is all very well to invite a few people to tea, but to invite over five thousand is a bit excessive, and at the end of the meal there are 12 baskets over (John 6:1-15)! In the marriage feast at Cana, when the wine runs out, Jesus produces another 160 gallons (John 2:1-12), mirroring the prodigality of God.

On the night before he died, Jesus, knowing that God had put everything into his hands and that he was returning to his Father, took water and a towel, and he washed his disciples' feet. How does God use his power? He uses it to serve, and so Jesus tells the disciples that they, too, must wash one another's feet (John 13:1-15). Then Jesus took a piece of bread, blessed it, broke it and gave it to his disciples saying, 'This is my body, given for you' (Luke 22:10). So this is what God is like, like a piece of bread broken, that we may have life.

When Jesus then said, 'Do this in memory of me,' he did not simply mean, 'Repeat this ritual for all time' but rather, 'This action is to be the pattern of your life, too.' You must be ready to be broken that others may live.

John tells us that when Jesus died on the cross, one of the soldiers took a lance and pierced his side, and there came out blood and water. John sees this as the water in which we are cleansed and redeemed.

■ MEETING GOD

Where are we to find this God of compassion, of tenderness, mercy and love? Jesus gives us a clue in his description of the Last Judgement (Matthew 25:31-46). It is an extraordinary passage, for we might expect Jesus to say something about prayer, worship and correct belief, but he does not. We will be judged, he says, by the way we have behaved towards one another, for it is in our treatment of one another that we meet God. 'I was hungry and you gave me food, I was thirsty and you gave me drink... lacking clothes and you clothed me.' And the people say, 'But when did we see you like this?' Jesus replies 'In so far as you did this to one of these least... you did it to me.' (Matthew 25:31-46)

So what is God like and where do we find him? He is a God of love and compassion, nearer to us than we are to ourselves, and we find him in the way we relate to others and to ourselves. The political, social and economic structures in which we live, the way we behave towards others, our friends, but also to strangers, are not questions extraneous to religion, but are of the very essence of our relationship to God. One writer has said, and I have a nasty suspicion he is right, that we are as near to God as we are the person we least like!

This leads us on to a further question. If this is what God is like, how are we to let God be God in us and through us?

■ EXERCISES FOR SECTION THREE

1. Is the God of this chapter attractive to you or repulsive or a bit of both?

• Concentrate on what you find attractive and speak to God simply from your heart.

• Now look at what you find uncomfortable and talk to God about that. Don't be afraid to grumble to God.

■ 4
KNOWING GOD

SO FAR, we have been thinking about God. But knowing God is very different from thinking or knowing about God. We can learn about God from books, sermons and lectures; we can only know God by meeting him ourselves. God is known by God alone. God alone can teach us what God is like, and the experience will be different for each of us, for God has made each of us unique.

Knowing God may be compared to knowing a close friend. Although we may have a detailed knowledge of our friend's curriculum vitae, which we can communicate to others, we cannot communicate the friendship itself, for the friendship goes beyond words. It consists of an inner knowing, an inner sharing, a sense of at-one-ness. It is a knowledge that colours everything we experience, for whatever we see or hear, whatever we think or feel, we experience not just with our own perception, but with our friend's perception as well, so that the breadth and intensity of our perception is increased.

■ SPENDING TIME WITH GOD

As in human friendship, we cannot come to know God unless we spend time with him. In one sense, this is a ridiculous statement, for whether we like it or not, we are with God all the time. However, if we are to come to know God for ourselves we need to put aside some time when we try to give him our full attention. As we do this we find that God expands our consciousness beyond its narrow confines of self-centred interest into an infinite expanse. What are we meant to do in the time we spend with God? The usual answer is 'pray', but it is not a very helpful answer because prayer spells boredom to many – sitting or kneeling in church, listening to other people's prayers, often in outmoded or unintelligible language, or expressing sentiments which sound exaggeratedly pious and bear little or no relation to life as we experience it.

But prayer means far more than this and there

are as many ways of praying as there are human beings. In this chapter I shall suggest a few ways of praying. They are not the ways you *ought* to pray, but ways that may get you started on your own way of praying, which will be different from mine or from anyone else's. Prayer is:

- a raising of the mind and heart to God
- a waiting
- a listening
- a conversation with God
- a being still
- a letting go and letting God
- being attentive
- being empty handed before God
- praise, thanksgiving, adoration

In all these descriptions, there is one essential attitude which belongs to every type of true prayer, that is an attitude of stillness before God.

■ BEING STILL

The psalmist says, 'Be still and acknowledge that I am God.' (Psalm 46:10) The reason why stillness is so important is that in all prayer it is God who prays in us. 'There is a sense in which we do not pray, can never pray. St Paul says that we cannot say, 'Abba' unless the Holy Spirit prays it in our hearts (see Romans 8:14-17). Notice that the descriptions of prayer given above all describe dispositions for prayer, rather than prayer itself. Even when our prayer is a conversation with God, it has to be a conversation, not a monologue; we have to listen, then speak as we feel prompted to speak. Jesus said, 'Do not babble as the gentiles do!' (Matthew 6:7)

Being still is also important for the reasons given in chapter 1, namely our tendency to create God in our own likeness, to impose our own ideas on God and then claim that they are God's, so causing havoc to ourselves and others while feeling very righteous.

Even when, intellectually, we realise that these are false images, emotionally the image may still affect us, making us, for example, reluctant to pray, either because we dislike God (Uncle George) or feel praying is unnecessary (a Santa Klaus God).

Many books have been written about ways of

praying. Here I am giving only a few outline suggestions. In the end, you will learn to pray by praying, not by reading countless books on the subject.

How to be still

It is difficult enough for most of us to remain physically still for any length of time; it is even more difficult to be still in our minds. As long as we are awake, our minds are constantly tugging our attention in some direction. However, if we concentrate our attention fully on what we are feeling, we cannot at the same time be thinking, so here is a simple exercise in being still, concentrating on what we are feeling.

Sit on a chair, your feet firmly on the ground, your back straight but not rigid, your hands joined or resting in your lap. You can also do this exercise lying on the floor or on your bed. Paul said, 'It is in him that we live, and move, and exist.' (Acts 17:28) We live enfolded within the goodness of God. So don't try to think about God, but just relax into the enfolding of God. Start from the top of your head and work downwards, relaxing all the muscles of your head, face, shoulders and so on down to your toes.

Focus your attention on the relaxing feeling. If you find thoughts are intruding, like, 'This doesn't seem to be helping me much to know God,' or, 'Must remember not to miss Coronation Street,' acknowledge the thoughts, but get straight back to relaxing. If you feel an itch or discomfort, acknowledge the itch, but don't move, and focus on the relaxing.

If you are a very busy and active kind of person you will think this type of exercise is a great waste of time. Waste time on it, and you will soon discover that in fact it is a most useful use of time.

However you may pray, it is always good to start with a relaxation exercise like this. A French poet, Charles Péguy, wrote a series of poems called 'God speaks'. In one of the poems God berates humankind. 'You are so busy,' says God, 'with things you consider important, and what none of you realises is that the most important thing you do in a day is go to sleep, because when you go to sleep you entrust yourselves to me and you wake up refreshed!' So begin with a relaxation exercise, then if you fall asleep, you can thank God when you wake.

As simple as a child

Once you feel relaxed, you may be ready for a conversation with God. Jesus said, 'Unless you become like little children you will never enter the kingdom of Heaven.' (Matthew 18:3) So in your conversation be as simple as a child and speak from the heart. The simpler the prayer, the better. It might be just, 'God help me', or, 'Let me know you', or, 'Show me your face'.

Review the day

Another simple form of prayer, especially suitable for the few minutes before you go to sleep, is a brief review of the day. You know how it is if you have had a fierce row during the day. Before you go to sleep you are still remembering the row: what he said, and she said, and how they were looking as they said it. You then remember what you said, and kick yourself for being so slow witted, because now you can think of the cutting remark that would have flattened your opponents!

Use this playback ability to pray with. Focus your attention on those moments of the day that you have enjoyed. Recall them, relish them for as long as you can, avoiding any self-approval or self-disapproval. Then thank God for those moments. They are gifts from God to you with love.

When you first do this exercise, you will probably be surprised at how many good moments there were in the day.

If you do this exercise once, it may make little difference, but if you do it regularly, it begins to change the way you perceive things, seeing more good moments in the day and appreciating them more. A man to whom I was giving a retreat came in one day looking even happier than usual. I commented on this and he said, 'I've just had a cup of coffee and it was the best cup I've ever had in my life, for I realised while drinking it that God was enjoying it in me!'

A short Bible passage

Another way of praying is to take a short passage of Scripture, the shorter the better. God is in all things, but for Christians the Scriptures are privileged writings, preserved by tradition because they believe that God speaks through the medium of these writings.

Read the passage slowly several times. Do not try to analyse it, or think how it applies to your own life, just read it. If you are on your own, read it aloud.

Notice any word or phrase that catches your attention. This is important. Our subconscious mind is often quicker than our conscious mind to recognise our real needs. That word or phrase has much to teach you, as you will realise if you give it your attention.

Focus your attention on the phrase. It may be a phrase like 'Don't be afraid', or 'I am with you', or 'You are precious in my sight and I honour you'. Just listen to it, avoiding any self-judgement.

You may find that thoughts and memories start coming into your mind, perhaps things or people you fear, or feelings of failure, of self-hate, or hate of someone else. Let the phrase hover over your fear, or sense of failure, or worthlessness, then talk to God from your heart.

Express your feelings of anger, bitterness or resentment. Trust that God is big enough to take your tantrums! No topic is forbidden and there is no thought or feeling that cannot become the substance of your prayer.

If you cannot express your feelings in words, try drawing them. Very often the drawing can say more than our conscious mind is aware of. If you are on your own you can also express your feelings in gestures, or mime, or dance.

Imagine the scene

Using our imaginations in prayer can help us to meet God. Gospel scenes are particularly suitable for imaginative prayer, but any passage of Scripture can be used.

First, read the passage until it is thoroughly familiar to you. Then imagine that the scene is happening at this moment and you are present, an active participant in it. You do not have to turn yourself into one of the characters: just be yourself. Talk with some of the characters in the scene and let them talk to you. Talk to Jesus and hear what he says to you.

You may think you have no imagination and that this prayer is not suitable for you. But everyone has imagination of some kind. It may not be very visual, but you can still have a sense of the scene.

Whatever happens through this exercise of the imagination, you can use it to help you to pray because imagination projects into our consciousness much that is going on subconsciously, influencing our perception, actions and reactions in ways of which we are not fully aware. If, for example, I am trying to picture a gospel scene but Jesus seems invisible, or distant, then that is probably reflecting a truth about myself. I may have professed belief in him and said prayers to him without facing up to the fact that he is not very real to me – that he is actually a distant, insubstantial figure. Once I have understood this, I can pray that he may become a reality to me.

The imaginative exercise has thus not been a failure, but has shown me more clearly my feeling of remoteness from Jesus and my need to pray at a greater depth, 'Lord, show me your face'.

■ WELL KNOWN PRAYERS

Other ways of praying include praying a well known prayer like the 'Our Father', praying it slowly, in rhythm with your breathing, or praying it phrase by phrase, spending as long as you like on any one phrase before moving on to the next one, never feeling that you have to finish the prayer.

Or you can pray a word or phrase repetitively, like the well known Jesus prayer, 'Lord, Jesus Christ, Son of the Living God, have mercy on me', or 'Come, Lord', or 'Show me your face'.

The purpose of repetitive prayer is to still the mind, so enabling you to become more open to the reality of God. But all that is only the beginning.

■ EXERCISE FOR SECTION FOUR

Practise the methods of prayer suggested, especially the stillness exercise.

Say to yourself: 'It is enough to keep my soul tranquil and quiet, like a child in its mother's arms, like a child that has been fed.' (Psalm 131)

So don't try too hard!

THE JOURNEY TO GOD

W<small>E GROW</small> in the knowledge of God, and there is no end to our growing. As St Paul writes to the Ephesians:

> 'May he, through his Spirit, enable you to grow firm in power with regard to your inner self, so that Christ may live in your hearts through faith, and then, planted in love and built on, with all God's holy people you will have the strength to grasp the length, the height and the depth, so that, knowing the love of Christ, which is beyond knowledge, you may be filled with the utter fullness of God. Glory be to him whose power, working in us, can do infinitely more than we can ask or imagine.'
>   (Ephesians 3:15–20)

That is why growing in the knowledge of God can be compared to a journey, and the church is called 'The Pilgrim People of God'.

■ ON PILGRIMAGE

Pilgrimage has been described as 'the poor person's substitute for mysticism'. The mystic has glimpses, which are a direct knowledge of God.

The rest of us are aware of an inner emptiness, an inner longing, which we cannot understand. We do not know what to do with it, so in order to clarify the confusion we externalise it by finding some holy place and going there on pilgrimage. Pilgrimage is a very useful exercise and teaches us many spiritual lessons. We realise on pilgrimage, especially if we are doing it on foot, that unless we really want to reach our destination we are unlikely ever to arrive, for weariness, exhaustion, or distractions on the way will divert us from our goal. We also realise that the journey can only be made one step at a time and that if we fail to take those steps we shall never arrive. And we have to learn to accept bad days and good days, difficult and steep stretches of the road as well as easy ones. On some days we feel full of energy; on others days we are limp and lethargic. If we reflect on these things we begin to see their application to our own inner life.

■ THE INNER JOURNEY

The inner journey is through our own consciousness, which consists of endless layers. At one stage of consciousness we may become aware of God, delight in him, experience great peace, strength and happiness. Then a crisis happens and we are thrown into confusion, doubt our former experience, begin to wonder whether God really does exist and feel trapped in our own hopelessness. It is good to know that this is part of the journey, so that we do not panic. It is also good to know that these difficult periods are God nudging us to change, to move nearer, to trust at a deeper level of consciousness.

God is in everything. There is no circumstance or state in which we can find ourselves where God is not. The Chinese have a character for crisis which represents both danger and opportunity. So whenever you find yourself in a crisis, know that it is an opportunity to grow.

> 'You must love the Lord your God with all your heart, with all your soul, with all your strength and with all your mind.'
> Luke 10:27

It is easy enough to say these words and even to assent to them with the surface part of our minds, but when our health is threatened, or we fail an exam, or lose our job, or are rejected by those we love, then turmoil starts within and we feel life is not worth living and there is nothing more to hope for. Our faith in God seems to have disappeared along with whatever it is we have lost.

If we then reflect for a moment, we can begin to see that God has not really been our rock, refuge and salvation, but that we have considered our health, or wealth, or reputation to be our rock, refuge and strength. Therefore we need to pray to God in our darkness and beg him to anchor us in his goodness alone.

■ A PRACTICAL TEST

At every moment of our existence God is drawing us to be at one with him, with ourselves and with all creation and, whether consciously or unconsciously, we are always responding with a 'yes' or a 'no'. To get in touch with this truth, here is a simple exercise to try at night after you have reviewed the day and thanked God for the good moments.

Pray for enlightenment so that you may become more aware of God drawing you. Then look at your moods during the day, without analysing them or making any judgements about them. Our moods and feelings come from our desires. When our desires are satisfied, we are in a good mood; when they are frustrated, we are in a bad mood. So the point of looking at our moods is to get in touch with our desires. What do you really desire? Is it to know, love and serve God, to act justly, love tenderly, be true and compassionate? Or do you desire that all creation should praise, reverence and serve you?

When you have looked at your moods, you can ask a simple question, 'Whose kingdom, God's or mine, are my moods indicating?' For example, if I feel utterly devastated because someone has criticised me publicly, why am I so shattered – is it because God's kingdom has been damaged, or my personal kingdom?

This exercise can give us self-knowledge, which is the beginning of wisdom, and helps us to see the split in our own spirituality. We may profess the love of God with our lips, but our moods show us the true state of affairs. Express your sorrow to God if you find you have been centred on your kingdom, not his, knowing that he always forgives, and beg him to keep you centred on His kingdom tomorrow.

■ 'WE ARE LEGION'

In the Gospels, Jesus heals the Gerasene demoniac (Mark 5:1-20). It is a most useful healing miracle to ponder imaginatively. No matter how bad you may be feeling, you are unlikely to have reached the depths of the demoniac who lives among the tombs. He is in such inner torment that all night and all day he howls and gashes himself, and nothing can constrain him, neither fetters nor chains. When Jesus asks him his name, with great insight he answers, 'Legion, for there are many of us.'

In all of us there are innumerable desires and urges, appetites and emotions, all conflicting, some of them in our consciousness, but more in our subconscious.

The first time I watched the television programme 'One Man and his Dog', I found it an excellent image of our human psyche. The whole operation depends upon the relationship between the sheepdog and the shepherd. If the relationship is good, then the sheepdog will bring the sheep together and drive them into the sheepfold. If the relationship is not good, then however intelligent and fast the dog, the whole operation will fail.

The sheep correspond to the various desires, appetites, longings and emotions within us. The sheepdog corresponds to the deepest part of ourselves, 'the fine point of the soul', as St Francis of Sales calls it. This is the part of us which expresses what we really desire in the depths of ourselves. It is good to ask ourselves, what do I really want in the depth of myself? It is not an easy question to answer because we desire so many different things.

A useful exercise is to imagine you have died and someone writes your obituary notice. What would you like to be said of you? That you never lost an argument in your life, or that you made the most money in the shortest time and became the biggest tycoon in history? Would

you like to be known as someone who was
transparently honest, courageous and generous,
who brought life and laughter to all you met?

Try writing out your own obituary. Don't
write the obituary you are afraid you might have,
but the obituary that, in your wildest dreams,
you would love to have.

This exercise can put you on track of what
you really desire. If we could discover what the
best and deepest part of us really desires, we
would be on the way to finding out God's will,
for God's will is our life, our happiness, our
fulfilment. In all prayer we should try to pray out
of this deepest part of ourselves and not allow the
more superficial parts, which are usually the most
noisy, to deter us. It is only in so far as the
deepest part of ourselves grows strong and God-
centred that we shall be able to control, order
and gain strength from the destructive urges and
emotions within us, which threaten to tear us
apart and can make us feel like 'Legion'.

■ 'DON'T BE AFRAID!'

If you wish to find God in everything, the most

important and fundamental attitude you can have is the attitude of trust. That is why, in the Scriptures, the most common phrase uttered by God is, 'Don't be afraid', and the next most common phrase is, 'I am with you'. It is in trusting that we learn to trust.

Faith is not primarily about believing doctrines, nor is it believing that there is a God out there. Faith is an attitude of trust in whatever circumstances we find ourselves. It is trusting that God is in these facts, however painful and unpleasant they may be, and that if we turn our attention to him, he will reveal himself to us as the God of a love and goodness which goes beyond anything we can think or imagine.

■ FANTASY OR REALITY?

If we try to know God and practise trust, how do we know it is God that we have found and not an idealised version of ourselves? How can we be sure we have not fallen into the trap discussed in chapter 1, of making God in our own image.

If it really is God whom we have found, then our minds and hearts will be seized by the compassion of God and we shall have a greater and keener sense of our identification with other people. We will feel more for them and with them, and serving them will be a delight, not a grim obligation. The God whom we serve is a God of peace, tranquillity and strength, a God whom we serve is a God of peace, tranquillity and strength, a God of delight, and our soul will know this, as St Paul did, even if we are persecuted, discounted, in pain and afflicted by weakness.

■ EFFECTING CHANGE

When we look at our world, its pain and suffering, and then at ourselves and our inability to do anything about it, we can become overwhelmed by our own helplessness and powerlessness. A good question then to ask ourselves is, 'Who do you think you are?' Our feelings of helplessness arise because we assume that we are the ones who should be able to effect lasting change; and we are leaving God out. But our Christian faith is faith in a God who, in Jesus, has entered into human suffering, human sinfulness, human death, and is risen again. God's love has triumphed over evil and can transform it into good. The only thing we can change is ourselves, and the only thing in ourselves that we can change is our way of perceiving reality.

In this little book we have asked the question, 'What is your God like?' He is the God 'whose power, working in us, can do infinitely more than we can ask or imagine.' (Ephesians 3:20) Whenever you fell helpless, or hopeless, turn to God, whose power is always revealed in weakness, so that St Paul could say, 'It is when I am weak that I am strong' (2 Corinthians 12:10).

■ EXERCISE FOR SECTION FIVE

Draw up a list in two columns, one headed 'Events that deaden me' and the other, 'Events that enliven me'.

Fill in these lists, including everything – people, places, activities, work, but especially ways of thinking and feeling about yourself. Keep adding to the list as things occur to you.

Look at the lists in the light of the truth that God is a God of life and love. God wants you to enjoy his creation, and your full humanity is God's glory.

Wolf Baby

It was supposed to be a big adventure. Tom and Ellie were really excited to be visiting Louis in the Scottish Highlands. Louis had been pen pals with Tom and Ellie Tyler for three years: they were great friends by letter, but this was the first time they'd met. Everyone was very nervous - especially Tom and Ellie as they picked up their bags and stood by the door...

The train came to a stop in front of a sign which said: `INCHMULLEN – Dumfries & Galloway Region`. Even at first glance, it seemed like a small town in the middle of nowhere.

"Look!" said Ellie, "there's Louis now!" She and Tom started waving. Louis, a rather small and anxious-looking boy with straight dark hair, waved back.

Louis' father, Grant Garou, opened the carriage door. Unlike his son, Mr Garou was a huge man with strong hairy arms and a shaggy black beard. He stared at the Tyler children with bright, sharp eyes. Ellie noticed anger in them and perhaps a little fear too, which she thought was rather odd.

Tom rather shyly said hello. Ellie smiled at Louis. "It's lovely to meet you at last," she said, her voice shaking slightly.

"Yes," Mr Garou answered in a growly kind of voice.

"We'll see…"

Louis glanced at his father uncertainly and said nothing.

Mr Garou walked ahead with the bags and the children followed. Ellie couldn't help but notice that all of the people stopped to stare at them. 'As though we're strange, and not just strangers…' she thought uneasily.

They came out through the station entrance into bright autumn sunlight. Mr Garou's truck was parked close by. Louis had said in his letters that his father was a forester and spent days away working in the vast pine timberlands surrounding the town.

Ellie gasped at the wonderful, breathtaking scenery. In the distance, tall mountains reached to the sky. Down in the wide valley, Inchmullen was a cluster of buildings following the river. It was all so sunny, so open – and yet the people seemed very dark and shadowy, not happy at all.

Tom pointed out another town that was some miles away in the distance.

"Oh, that's Castle Rock," Louis explained. "Perhaps we'll go there soon to shop! And look –"

He indicated a colourful patch close to the river. "The funfair's come to town! Maybe..." Then he stopped, looked anxiously at his father again, and became silent.

They piled into Mr Garou's truck and headed for home. Passing through the town's main street, the children noticed a huge coloured poster nailed to a fence...

JEREMIAH DARK'S FUNFAIR AND TRAVELLING SHOW.

ROLL UP! ROLL UP! SEE THE AMAZING VAMPIRE BOY.

THE ASTONISHING REPTILE WOMAN.

THE LIVING MUMMY FROM ANCIENT EGYPT THE HUMAN SPIDER...

AND A NEW ADDITION - THE WOLFBABY!

PLUS YOUR FAVOURITE RIDES AND GAMES...

ROLL UP! ROLL UP! ROLL UP!!

Mr Garou snarled angrily. "Do you see what they're doing, son?" he barked at Louis. "They're making fun of people who are different from themselves. It's disgusting! It should be stopped!"

Tom and Ellie looked shocked at this outburst. Louis just hung his head in dismay...

***

"I think we got off to a bad start," Ellie muttered, as she and Tom left their bedroom and started down the stairs.

It was an hour later. They had met Louis` mother – a kindly lady, but as quiet and as secretive as everyone else in Spring Falls. And after a meal, they asked if they could explore for themselves. Mr Garou grunted a reply. "But don't wander too far and make sure you're back by nightfall..."

"Can Louis come with us?" Ellie asked hesitantly.

"It's not safe –"Mrs Garou started to say.

Her husband glanced at her quickly. "No, he can not. Louis has some jobs to do around the house. You go – but remember what I said..."

"Well I hope the rest of the visit isn't going to be like this!" Tom muttered unhappily to his sister.

They reached the bottom of the stairs and were just about to walk to the door, when they heard Louis' voice coming from the kitchen. He sounded terribly upset.

"I did the wrong thing, didn't I? I shouldn't have invited them," he said with a little sob of sadness.

"No, son. I think you did the right thing, but maybe at the wrong time... We have tried to keep the world out for long enough. Times are changing. But it's hard not to be frightened of people. After all, they'd be frightened of us..."

Someone knocked gently at the back door. Mrs Garou answered it. Several men were standing there. They were all big, like Louis' Dad, and all had shaggy beards and long hair. They came in silently, towering over Louis and filling the room.

Mr Garou spoke solemnly. "Well, you've all seen that so-called 'funfair', with its specimens and freaks – and now little Harriet Brandner is missing. So, I guess we all know what must be done."

One of the men, who had reddish hair and a wide, angry grin, leaned forward across the table. "Yes, Grant, we're with you... Will it be tonight?"

"Yes tonight," Grant Garou agreed gruffly. "Before the fair moves on."

The red-haired man said, "And what about the human children, little Louis' friends?"

They all stared at Louis, who gazed back, wide-eyed and frightened

"Let's just hope they don't get in the way," Mr Garou told them softly.

Tom and Ellie held their breath as they listened from the stairs. Now, as they let out a shuddering sigh, Ellie looked unsurely at her brother.

"What's going on, Tom? What does he mean, `human children`?"

Tom frowned in puzzlement and fear. "I'm not sure..."

A shadow loomed in the hall and they both jumped.

Louis came through from the kitchen, instantly realising his two friends had heard everything.

"I can't explain, not yet," he said. "But please trust me. No one will hurt you if you stay out of the way."

Louis dug into his pocket and pressed something into Tom's hand; a strange silver coin with the face of a wolf stamped upon it.

"What's this?" Tom asked. He had never seen anything like it before.

Louis shook his head. "Never mind what it is. Just keep it with you. And if anything unusual happens, hold it high in the air. Then you'll be safe."

And before the children could question him further, Louis returned to the kitchen and shut the door behind him.

***

Ellie and Tom could see plenty of people going to the fair from Castle Rock. But no one, apart from themselves, was walking along the road out of Inchmullen.

"What's going on?" Ellie muttered, shaking her head at the mystery.

"And who's Harriet Brandner? "Tom wondered as he glanced again at the silver coin Louis that had given them. "Do you suppose she's been kidnapped?"

Ellie was about to reply, but then both of them froze as they heard an eerie, soulful sound echoing through the trees nearby.

"What?" Tom said, startled. His sister's eyes went wide with fright.

As the children listened, the sound came again. Tom and Ellie turned towards the huge dark forest spreading over the hills.

And for a third time the weird sound echoed around them.

Ellie's mouth quivered. "T-Tom...That howling it's..."

"I know," Tom whispered fearfully. "It's the howling of wolves!"

***

They hurried on towards the bright lights of the funfair. It felt safer being closer to all the noise and crowds except when Tom looked back along the road and saw a huge full moon rising above Inchmullen. By its light, watching them from the roadside, was a great red-furred wolf...

He said nothing, not wanting to frighten Ellie further. Besides, she was becoming more cheerful as they arrived at the funfair.

They had a turn on the coconut shy and the dodgem cars. Then Ellie insisted they try the helter-skelter. After that, Tom wanted a hot dog. Then they both bought a cola, before riding on the carousel.

At last, bright-faced and giggling, they turned a corner and found themselves in a much quieter part of the fair. There were no crowds here, just rows of caravans and trailers, some empty cages and boxes stacked on top of each other.

Ellie's smile slowly faded. "We came the wrong way, Tom. This is the back of the funfair."

She paused as a mournful squeal drifted eerily through the air, then pointed towards a shabby tent nearby. "It's coming from there..."

"That must be where they keep the human spider and the vampire boy!" There was excitement in Tom's voice.

Ellie looked at her brother seriously. "That's what Mr Garou hated so much. All those poor things locked up for people to stare at. It isn't right."

"I'll bet they're fakes anyway, "Tom replied with a sneer. "I think they're all just be dummies or dolls."

"Well let's find out," Ellie told him, "and put our minds at rest!"

They walked between two huge trailers to the front of the tent. A bored looking man sat at the entrance. Ellie paid for herself and Tom and they went inside.

The lights were dim and the cages and display cases were half in shadow.

"I told you so." Tom pointed to 'The Reptile Man'. It was obviously built of papier mache, poorly painted to look like a monster. The 'Vampire Boy' also was nothing more than a taylor's dummy with silly plastic fangs stuck on. And ` The Human Spider` was made of rope tied around a badly painted doll....

Ellie smiled as they walked on. "OK Tom, you were right and I was..."

Then they came to the cage of ' The Wolfbaby '. And there, its tiny paws

gripped around the bars, knelt a tiny wolf-child with the saddest eyes the children had ever seen.

Ellie put her hand to her mouth to stifle a cry. "Oh Tom it's real...It really is a werewolf!"

The little creature cocked its head and opened its mouth. Its teeth were white and sharp and perfect. It whimpered pitifully.

"It's only a baby!" Tom was suddenly furious. His eyes were hot with tears and temper. "The poor thing's been taken from its parents and thrown in this cage and left... It's Jeremiah Dark who's the monster!" Tom shouted. "And I'm going to do something about it!"

"I bet this is Harriet Brandner!" said Ellie suddenly.

"Don't you see Tom, there must be a family of wolf-people living near Inchmullen and the rest of the townsfolk are trying to protect them!"

"But werewolves are wild and fierce and – and – they eat people, Ellie!"

"You've only read about that in books," Ellie said dismissively. "How do you know for sure – have you ever met a real werewolf?"

"Only this one." Tom gave a faint, wavering smile. "Though I'm not sure I'd want to meet her father."

Both children jumped as something loomed up from behind the were-baby's cage. Something huge, red-eyed and fierce.

A werewolf, twice the size of a man with teeth like knives. Its gigantic hands reached down and pulled the bars aside as though they were made of toffee. It snatched the tiny werewolf up, roared at Tom and Ellie then disappeared from sight.

In the next instant there was a commotion outside. Men were shouting and torchlights flickered around the tent.

Tom grabbed Ellie's hand. "Quick, follow me. We don't want to be blamed for this."

The huge werewolf had torn his way through the back of the tent. Tom led Ellie through the rip. They began running down the narrow space between rows of lorries and caravans.

Before they reached the end, a crowd of angry looking men blocked their way. One of them pointed.

"There, Jeremiah! There are the thieves!"

The men, armed with sticks and firebrands, charged forward.

"This way!" Ellie hissed. She dragged Tom under a parked lorry and out the other side. The way was clear –

Until suddenly three massive werewolves jumped down from the top of the lorry and surrounded them.

Ellie shrieked, and Tom's heart gave a great leap of fright. There was no escape.

The wolves closed in, their jaws gaping wide, their red tongues panting, their eyes glinting in the moonlight like polished coins.

Coins, Tom thought, suddenly remembering. Polished coins!

He pulled Louis' silver coin from his pocket and held

it high.

"Don't hurt us," he said loudly. "We don't mean you any harm."

One of the beasts growled something. The others nodded their great shaggy heads.

And before Tom and Ellie could do anything further, two werewolves had scooped them up on their backs.

The powerful creatures, with the children clinging desperately to their long fur, ran as fast as a speeding car under the moonlit sky; away from the funfair and the shouting men, through the dark forest, and into Inchmullen.

They went straight to the square at the end of the main street. And there the people of the town were waiting.

And all of them were werewolves.

At the front of the crowd Grant Garou stood and watched. His teeth glinted. Nearby, a female wolf nestled the werebaby in her arms. It seemed contented at last.

Only Louis was in his human shape. He looked worried as Tom and Ellie were gently lowered to the ground by the werewolves.

"Harriet is safe now," he said. Grant Garou nodded.

"Nobody will come for her now," he said. He was changing even as he spoke, his wolf-shape melting away.

There followed a few seconds of silence, then Louis held out his hands. "So now you know our secret..." As he spoke, his body seemed to shiver and change. And he too stood in his wolf-shape, silver and black.

"We are in your power," Grant Garou added, his great shaggy coat sliding back fully into his body. "If people like Jeremiah Dark found out about us, he would try to put us all in cages!"

The crowd murmured and growled, a low, nervous sound.

"We have lived here for so long," Louis went on. "Keeping ourselves to ourselves. And we have been so frightened. Mankind has mistrusted us for centuries; hunted us down. We just want to live in peace..."

Ellie smiled. "We won't tell on you, honestly. Will we, Tom?"

"No," Tom agreed, "we'd never do that. We understand now that not all werewolves are fierce and evil."

"And neither are you!" Louis chuckled, becoming a small, shy boy once more.

Ellie went and gave him a hug.

Tom strode up to Grant Garou, who grinned, reached down and gripped Tom's fingers in his vast, black-clawed paw.

And they shook hands, as equals and friends.